The most essential and valuable tool in a pilot's flight bag is MzeroA.com its required for all my students
- Larry Diamond CFII

MzeroA.com, Publisher

Cover Design: MzeroA.com

© 2019-20 by MzeroA.com

Proudly printed in the United States of America

ISBN: 9781798744833

CONTENTS

ACKNOWLEDGMENTS

This book was a collaborative effort by the MzeroA.com team,- some of the smartest and certainly most dedicated aviators I know.

ABOUT THE AUTHOR

Jason Schappert is a full-time flight
instructor at MzeroA.com with over
10,000 hours of flying experience.
His videos have been viewed by
millions of pilots all across the world
and his Online Ground School has
helped created over 12,000 pilots in
the past 3 years alone.

MzeroA.com was named to the INC 500 list of fastest
growing private companies in 2017 & 2018.

CHAPTER 1
GETTING STARTED

"THERE ARE 3 THINGS THAT DO YOU NO GOOD
IN AVIATION...ALTITUDE ABOVE YOU, RUNWAY
BEHIND YOU, AND FUEL ON THE GROUND."

- PILOT WISDOM

WHAT IS A PRIVATE PILOT CERTIFICATE?

A private pilot is someone who holds an aviation license that is limited to flying solely for pleasure trips or simply to just enjoy the sky above our heads. Private pilots cannot fly for compensation or hire.

Whether flying as a hobby or as a pathway to a future career, everyone starts with their private pilot certificate (*with the exception of sport pilot- more on this later.*)

In order to become a private pilot, you'll need to complete a ground school, find a flight school and meet the FAA minimums outlined below:

- 40 hours of flight time

- 10 hours solo

- 20 hours of instruction

That's just a VERY basic overview of the 40 hours listed above. There are many areas of knowledge and skill that must be gained such as night flying, cross country flights, test prep, etc...

Let me also be real with you though: Very few people complete their private pilot training near the FAA minimum of 40 hours. In fact, the national average for earning a private pilot certificate is 79 hours! Almost DOUBLE the "FAA Minimum." The term FAA Minimum means just that. It is the bare-bones minimum that is required for application for a checkride *(the big final exam)*.

The tasks, skills and knowledge required for the private pilot checkride must be performed in a safe and efficient manner. Each student will require different amounts of time to accomplish the FAA minimums.

A WORD OF CAUTION:

This is getting a bit ahead of myself but be aware that when flight schools talk prices and market their services to you, with comments like, "Oh, by the way a pilot certificate can be as inexpensive as $5,000!" take note that those numbers might be based on the FAA Minimum of 40 hours. They're not lying because it legally could be done in 40 hours; they're just being crafty marketers. Be aware!

I'm not saying that you can't complete your certificate in less than 50 hours. In fact, I've got a great system that I'm going to share with you in this book that helps save time and money during your training. It is going to help you take dozens of extra flight training hours off that bill while maximizing the hours spent on ground and flight training. More on this later.

MAKING THE RIGHT CHOICE

Believe it or not these next two decisions - choosing a flight school and choosing an instructor - can make or break your training.

Too often I see new pilots drive to a flight school, meet the first CFI (Certificated Flight Instructor) they see, and say "you're it. Let's go!"

You need to realize that you'll be spending thousands of dollars and dozens of hours of your time at this flight school with your designated instructor. They should be working for your business, not the other way around! **You** are the_employer and **they** are your employees.

Here are a few things any prospective student should look for and ask before making the leap with a flight school:

1. What kind of training aircraft does this school offer? This plays directly into your budget. Maybe they only have newer Cessna 172's when your wallet is on a Cessna 150 budget. Trust me: When I started out I wanted to fly that beautiful brand new Cessna 172 but my wallet could only afford the 1962 Cherokee 140.

N6711J: A 1962 Cherokee 140 and the plane that got it all started for Jason

2. How do the training aircraft look? I'll be honest... I'm not a very handy person. But when it comes to flying in airplanes I'm a pretty good judge. "If the owner lets the outside look like this (paint chipping, moldy smell

inside, corrosion on bare aluminum) I can take a pretty good guess on what other corners have been cut on the real important stuff... LIKE THE ENGINE! Ask to look at the aircraft maintenance logs. I recommend asking to see how they keep track of the 100 hour/ annual inspections. I know this sounds like a lot but this is your hard earned money that you are investing.

3. How many *operational* training aircraft does the school have? If there is only one Cessna 152 and there are 20 students, it will be difficult to schedule the airplane during a time when you can fly.

4.Is the airport/school close to home? Studies have shown that students are more likely to finish their training if the flight school is located within a 30 minute drive!

5.Is the airport non-tower or tower controlled and how busy is the airport?

The next section takes this a bit further.

WHAT MAKES A <u>GREAT</u> FLIGHT INSTRUCTOR?

No decision you make in your training is more important than choosing your flight instructor. Take it from me, I've had every CFI problem you could imagine, from a CFI telling me to "give up - you're not meant to fly" to the GREAT CFIs that make every hour count.

Before you select your CFI make sure they pass the MzeroA.com CFI Interview I've outlined below.

- *Do your schedules match?* For example, I am a weekday flyer. I enjoy taking my weekends off to spend time with friends and family so I would not be a good candidate for a student who can ONLY fly weekends

- *Do you know their goals?* I WISH someone would have told me to ask my CFI what his/her goals were. It would have saved me time and money during my commercial pilot certificate when I switched CFIs *eight* times! This was back in 2004 - 2005 when the airlines were hiring like crazy! If I had known that the CFIs I had chosen were sitting in a hiring pool waiting for Delta or United to call, I would have continued my search for an instructor who was dedicated to instructing. Because once they got that call, they were gone and I was stuck with a new CFI who knew NOTHING about me. I had to retrace my steps for each new instructor.

• *Find out the numbers!* How many students does this prospective CFI have? Eight is about the maximum load a full time CFI can handle at any one time and cut that in half for a part time CFI (this is speaking from experience). You don't want to get lost in the shuffle and have future scheduling issues so solve this early on.

• *What score, on average do their students get on the written test?* The minimum score to pass the FAA Written test is 70%. However who wants to just get by? Find this average score out!

• The question no CFI should hesitate to answer: *"What is your student pass rate?"* Chances are it's above 80%. For an instructor, a pass rate under 80% means that the FAA will seek you out to find out "what's up?" The FAA will recommend recurrent training for the CFI that has a higher than average flunk rate. I still proudly boast a 100% pass rate for both my personal Ocala, Florida based and online students. Knowing that below 80% is a red flag for unsatisfactory teaching, you can begin to make some decisions on your choice of instructor. Maybe your CFI hasn't put anyone up for checkride yet and you'll be their first. There's nothing wrong with that, but just be ready as you're somewhat of a guinea pig. Also realize you may be the first in a long line of students taught by a great instructor.

• *Is the CFI accountable and responsible?* What do I mean by this? The CFI is responsible for teaching you to be a safe and efficient pilot. To be able to take family and friends to wonderful places in an airplane. It's a tremendous responsibility for the CFI to ensure they impart a great amount of knowledge, experience and skill to their students. The CFI should also be held accountable for the quality of teaching given to their students. You want a CFI who strives and thrives with the student's progress. The CFI will seek out all resources, from other CFIs, books and the

FAA, to make the student's dream of the private pilot certificate a reality. If you think this sounds impossible, let me tell you it IS POSSIBLE. For some of us it takes longer, but there are some fantastic CFIs out there that are born to teach.

• *What's their reputation like?* Pilots are unlike any other demographic on earth. They like to talk. (Desperate Hanger Pilots Season 12 Coming To A Town Near You! Corny joke - sorry.) My point is that you'll have no problem asking around the airport and finding current students of the prospective CFI. If the CFI is good, he will have a list of past students as reference for you to get in contact with.

• *What's their teaching style?* We all learn differently. For myself, I'm a hands-on (kinesthetic) kind of learner. You might be more of a visual learner, a reader, etc. Find out how your CFI teaches and make sure it matches your learning style. A great CFI should also be able to adapt to you. If you are an engineer, the CFI should be able to use examples that you can relate to in teaching you about flight. If you work in healthcare, a CFI should be able to use relevant health-related examples to explain how the engine works, perhaps how the cylinder is like a syringe..

• *Can we take a discovery flight?* Just like you test drive a car, you should check out not only your prospective CFI and their teaching style but also the training aircraft. A discovery flight should be an option at any airport you go to. Expect to spend less than $150 to make it happen. It will be worth it.

One last note on this item and then I feel we can put the flight school/CFI debate to rest. Realize that you'll be spending dozens of hours with this person you choose to be your CFI. Please take the time to make the right choice as I've outlined above.

Need help making that decision a little easier?

We actually have a list of MzeroA.com approved flight schools and instructors who already meet a lot of the above criteria I mentioned. You can view that list online by going to:

FindACFI.com

HOW MUCH SHOULD I EXPECT TO PAY?

There's no getting around the fact that learning how to fly will be fairly expensive. To be honest, you have to be ready with upwards of $6,000 to sometimes $10,000 dollars if you are going to seriously pursue your certificate.

Let me make one very clear point. Two things hold you back in your flight training: Time and money.

If you feel money might be an issue, it would be wise to begin to save, budget, and set aside money for your flight training fund.

The range I mentioned above is an all-inclusive price. It takes into account the plane rental, fuel, instructor, ground school, books, examiner fees, etc.

Jason,

You're a great example for GA Pilots. You love what you are doing, love helping others, and enjoying the experience. Being a positive person myself, I'm glad I found you on the internet years ago when I started flying. I'm going for my commercial ticket now working towards my CFI, so the learning is just beginning, but like you say "A Good Pilot, is ALWAYS Learning.

Safe Flying,

Mike King

CHAPTER 2
HOW TO SAVE MONEY ON YOUR FLIGHT TRAINING

"THE ONLY TIME YOU HAVE TOO MUCH FUEL IS
WHEN YOU'RE ON FIRE!" - PILOT WISDOM

TIME & MONEY

As mentioned in the last chapter, no two things will be of a greater burden to you in your flight training than time and money.

Sometimes just one of those factors will play a role and in a worst case scenario, both will. What you'll realize in this chapter and during your flight training is that the saying "time is money" is in its truest form in aviation.

I ask my students a question when they are taking a discovery flight: "What makes airplanes fly?" They will come back with a snappy answer like wind, lift and the engineers will discuss Mr. Bernoulli. I laugh and say the answer is **MONEY**. Money is what makes airplanes fly.

The latest data on why students do not complete their training tells us that students fail due to poor training and, most of all, running out of money. It is so frustrating to see a student progressing through their training, gaining experience, having fun, being efficient and then run of money.

In this chapter I'll share with you some of my best-kept secrets to saving money during your flight training.

CHAIR FLYING

I once heard my very good friend Eric Crump, the director of aerospace at Polk State College say, "The airplane is a terrible classroom." It's a phrase I use to this day.

That phrase is spot on! As student pilots, we just want to go fly! Yet we don't realize that the airplane is for demonstrating what we know and to polish our aviation skills. As a classroom, the airplane stinks. You cannot pull over to a cloud, park the aircraft at 3,000 feet and go over steep turns on a notepad. That's like driving a stick shift car, texting, listening to NPR, talking to the significant other while driving at 70 miles per hour down the interstate. Remember that.

That is why I teach the art of chair flying.

Picture this with me. You're sitting back in your big comfy lazy boy chair, you close your eyes and begin to run through your power on stall procedures:

> "After I perform my clearing turns I'm
> going to begin to slow the airplane down to its
> takeoff rotation speed. Maintain my heading and
> altitude. I'm trying not to fixate on my airspeed
> indicator as I scan my instruments and look
> outside. Once I slow to my rotation speed I
> smoothly apply full power allowing that nose to
> come up. I glance at my turn coordinator briefly
> to make sure I'm keeping that airplane
> coordinated and holding my heading. As the
> nose continues upward I can feel the controls
> getting sloppy. I can now hear the stall warning
> horn. There is the buffeting. There is the break.
> Nose down, wings level, nose slowly back to level
> and airplane is back to cruise."

That is chair flying. Visualize yourself practicing each maneuver. You should show up to the airport having chair flown every maneuver you're going to do that day. Chair flying works especially well with landings and pattern work!

Chair flying doesn't have to be limited to your big comfy chair. It could be done in the airport parking lot, right before bed, or during breakfast. It doesn't matter when you do it. All that matters is that you take action to do it. (Do not do chair flying while driving. If something happens, like a ticket or accident, the police officer will not accept, "you know, Officer Jones, I was practicing my power on stalls when I was changing lanes." Not acceptable and not safe.)

I mean it when I tell you that if you don't get ANYTHING else out of this book, this tip alone will save you a few hundred dollars.

PRE & POST FLIGHT BRIEFS

Every CFI should give their student a detailed pre- and post- flight brief. THIS IS MANDATORY. I am seeing more and more CFIs slowly walk away from a lesson not even giving their students as much as a "good job" anymore.

Conducting a brief before and after your flight is another great way to save money on your flight training. Here's how.

The Preflight Brief

Before each and every flight you and your CFI should sit down and talk about what I call the "2 Ws"

- **Weather** - What's the weather like? Chances are your CFI might have already flown that day. He might have a take, a true pilot report, on what's happening up there versus what the airport is reporting. Are we even able to go flying? Do any of the predetermined conditions exceed your personal minimums? If everything checks out, continue onto the final "W"

- **What We're Doing Today** - You and your CFI did a post flight brief on the last flight. You already know that answer but it's always good to bring it up again with your CFI. You can chair fly the maneuver out loud with he/she sitting there to offer any further critique or recommendations.

When I do this with my students I go as far as to tell them, "Hey it looks like we'll be departing runway 23. Off of runway 23, we'll be making a left turn out to the south practice area where we'll start with our steep turns.

Don't you think this would be beneficial to you? When you're walking outside to preflight you can be visualizing that radio call, that take off, those steeps turns. Do not visualize during your preflight as you might miss something important. When I started doing these detailed briefs with my students the quality of our lessons soared!

The Post Flight Brief

The post-flight brief, by its nature, takes a little bit

longer. It's also where you'll get the best nuggets of knowledge from the day's lesson and future lessons.

I found that when I gave students instant feedback in the cockpit they acknowledged it but when I brought it up on the ground they would say things like "Oh yeah, thats a great point!" As if it was the first time they had ever heard it. This again strengthens the position that the airplane is a terrible classroom.

So while I still give that feedback in the cockpit I make a point to mention it after the flight. There is so much going on during a flight for a new student pilot that the knowledge retention rate while flying is quite low. So after each flight we play "Monday morning quarterback" and run through each phase of the flight.

This may sound a little different, but I ask the students to critique themselves. This gives the instructor an idea of what the students were thinking. I never ask yes or no questions. I had one student who was very respectful of teachers. He would say yes to everything I asked. I could have asked if the sun set in the East and he would have answered yes. So, since he was one of my first group of students, I learned to never ask yes or no questions except if they are feeling ill in the airplane. I ask very open questions that make them think in a very constructive way. The hardest judge each of us has is ourself. This will also help the instructor understand what they are doing well and what they need to tweak.

With my students, we go all the way back to the first takeoff and mention everything we did. Here is a quick example of a recent flight I did with a student.

"Your takeoff was awesome. You really did a great job of holding that centerline and I love the fact that you remembered to look over your shoulder at that runway to make sure we're flying that extended centerline straight out, as opposed to our last lesson.

You got us into the practice area, made our radio calls and did the clearing turns without me asking. This is HUGE! Remember flight training is all about a transfer of responsibility and you're really starting to be that "Pilot in Command." I like it.

We entered into steep turns to the left first and that one was spot on. However the one to the right needed a little bit of work. It was as if you were just a half second behind the airplane. Remember, steep turns are a visual maneuver, look outside, slice that nose across the horizon, and use a little bit of trim to help you with that yoke. There is no need to muscle the airplane through the sky..."

That post-flight debrief continues on but you get the picture. It is a recap infused with constructive criticism.

We complete the recap, answer any questions, then share with the student what's next. Knowing what to study and prepare for before your next lesson is invaluable to the learning process.

I will tell the student that the next lesson is going to be slow flight, steep turns, and stalls. The student can then go home and chair-fly those maneuvers thus making our time together and in the air ten times more productive.

Early on in my flight training, I unfortunately never received these kinds of briefs. I was made aware of what we were doing that day as I reached 3,000ft! Talk about a missed opportunity. The first time I even heard the term "slow flight" was when my CFI showed it to me at altitude and asked me to follow along. Don't let your CFI walk away without giving you a proper pre- and post-flight brief.

MY #1 FLIGHT TRAINING TIP

I'm often asked what my number one tip would be for a budding or prospective student. That tip can be summarized into one simple sentence:

"Learn Everything You Can On The Ground"

It all goes back to what we just spoke about: The airplane is a terrible and expensive classroom. If you try to do all your flight training without completing some sort of ground school, you are doing yourself a disservice.

I have the statistics to backup the statement that "for every hour you spend on the ground, you save two hours in the air." Flying is the fun part. All pilots feel that way. From your quick one hour lesson each week, that costs you around $150 a pop you will gain some stick and rudder skills. All the while, topics like airspace, regulations, flight planning, textual/physical weather all loom over your shoulder as the written test and checkride nag you. Students cannot jump into a cockpit of a hurtling piece of machinery and know how, why, and what is happening to the aircraft. They must have a foundation of solid comprehension that can only be studied on the ground.

I was in this spot. I loved flying and met every hour/solo requirement for my checkride. Yet I neglected to take my written test and had never taken a ground school. When prepping for the written test I realized I knew NOTHING about aviation. So rather than taking my checkride, I took two months off from flying to focus on my ground studies. That's two months that I could have been a private pilot and two months I could have been working towards another rating. Because I neglected my ground studies, my written test of 77% was a glaring testament of my not studying.

Yes, the guy whose has written eight best selling aviation books and has made a career as an aviation educator only got a 77% on his private pilot written test - proof that I'm human too and that anyone can make a turn around. Don't do what I did and skip your ground training. You will pay for it in the long run.

As a quick side note, if you're enjoying this book and my style of "real world/plain english" teaching, then you may also enjoy the #1 rated Online Ground School, which I'd love for you to become a member of. I'll share more about this on page 48.

Dear Jason,

Becoming a private pilot has been a dream of mine for many years. Career and life got in the way many times, but in 2013 I discovered the MzeroA Online Ground School and my dream became a reality.

I finally had a way to learn in a system that was compatible with my career because your materials are set forth in modules that allowed me to attend the ground school when my schedule permitted. The Online Ground School is delivered with personality, fun, and passion, which is consistent with your feelings and devotion in aviation.

I could tell when we met in Oshkosh that General Aviation is a way of life and it shows in the genuine love for teaching new pilots, which I recall feeling during each module within the Online Ground School. I became a Private Pilot after just 40 hours of flying and never missed a step during the checkride. I put in the work, but this accomplishment was not possible without the MzeroA Online Ground School.

I owe you a tremendous personal debt for the support and passion that you bring to General Aviation. Thank you for making my dream come true.

I look forward to flying together when I come to Florida someday. Until then, my friend, please keep developing the Online Ground School for all of the students who follow because as you have taught us, "A Good Pilot Is Always Learning." That motto keeps us all humble and improving.

Best regards,

Mark Tilkens

Private Pilot - July 18, 2013

CHAPTER 3

COMMON STUDENT PILOT PITFALLS/ERRORS

"A GOOD PILOT IS ALWAYS LEARNING™"

- JASON SCHAPPERT

In my 8,000+ flight hours, I've seen a lot of the same silly mistakes repeated over and over by student pilots. I figured I should share them so you can go into your training a little bit smarter and equipped with the knowledge to overcome a few of these common student pilot errors. The biggest life experiences learned are from our mistakes.

"It is not so much what you do to get into trouble, it is how you get out of trouble that is important." Larry M. Diamond, MzeroA.com CFII, PharmD

CHECKLIST USAGE

A checklist in aviation is sort of like a "Honey Do" list or a reminder list. Ready to start the engine? Complete steps 1-15. If the engine still didn't start, try steps 16-18.

From preflight to every imaginable emergency, there is a checklist. I always joke with other CFIs that you can spot a new student pilot versus a student pilot with, say, 30 hours based on how they do their preflight.

The new student pilot follows the checklist to the letter. They complete the entire preflight with checklist in their hand and spend more time to complete the preflight. Bravo to them as this kind of muscle memory will save their bacon some day.

The pilot with a few more hours leaves the checklist on the dashboard, conducts the entire thing from memory, and speeds through it all in hopes of getting flying sooner. Fact: We are easily distracted and our brains are the cause. This will cause our memory or recall to skip over stuff. We need checklists to make sure we do not miss anything on our preflight.

Your checklist has all the necessary steps (reminders) to do a proper preflight. I fully understand you might have an idea of how to preflight. After almost 4,000 hours in my Cessna 150 alone, I'm pretty sure I know my way around a preflight. Yet I still consult the checklist.

The only checklists that should be memorized are

your emergency procedures. These can be easily burned into your brain by doing what I call "flow checks." It is all based on muscle memory (see the image below.)

These emergency checklists are created in such a way that you can easily work a "flow" to verify the checklist components if time permits.

CLEARING TURNS

Before EVERY flight maneuver you conduct something called "clearing turns." You will scan three hundred and sixty degrees of sky in your area to make sure no obstacles or other aircraft are a potential hazard.

This is another one of those procedures that student pilots start out in the beginning doing so well then slowly work away from. I understand it's a "big sky" as some pilots call it. Having seen many near misses, I never forget to do my clearing turns.

A proper clearing turn is a standard rate turn (15 degrees of bank) always to the left first. Why always to the left? Because in a perfect world, if an airplane were passing or overtaking you from behind, it's instructed to do so off your right side and you want to avoid blindly turning into anyone.

You make that standard rate left turn 90 degrees to the left of your original heading, looking above below and all around for traffic and hazards. Once confirmed clear you lift the other wing and begin the same turn but to the right this time all the way back to your original heading.

OVERCONFIDENCE

You are instructed to be "The Pilot In Command," however there is a stark difference between **P**ilot **In Command** (PIC) and **D**angerous **U**nder-qualified **M**anic **B**ehind the controls (DUMB). Ok, that was a stretch - sorry!

My point is this: There is a fine line in aviation between confident and cocky. If you'd like to see a real world example of this in action, please take a look at the bonus webinar I did a while ago as part of my weekly webinar series held every week for my Online Ground

School members. I encourage you to set aside thirty minutes for this video.

Head Over To YouTube and Search

"MzeroA JFK Jr"

During the webinar I break down the JFK Jr Accident and you can see how the "chain of events" of an accident build.

Now don't misunderstand me, I want my student pilots to believe in themselves and their knowledge. I would NEVER solo a student if he/she didn't believe they could do it despite me thinking so. Pilots are confident and they are action takers but they need to manage their skills, emotions use their resources in a safe manner.

Again, I encourage you to set aside 30 mins and watch that video. It's that important.

KEEPING YOUR TRAINING ON TRACK

In flight training it can be so easy to get off track and drag it out longer than it should. A little background on my early days as a student:

All I did was fly. I didn't do ANY ground work but I could sure fly that airplane. That's all that matters right? Boy was I ever wrong!

I had met all the requirements to take my checkride except one, the **written test**. Needless to say, my training went from being ahead of schedule to two months behind schedule because it took me two months to get caught up to where I should be. I studied four to six hours a day during this period of time. Not only did I have a written test to prep for but also a checkride!

The route I wish I would have taken...

I wish someone would have grabbed me and shaken me saying "Do your ground work first!" So I'm going to be that guy for you.

1. No greater factor saves a student more money on their training than ground study. If I could do it all again, I would have completed an Online Ground School (learn more on page 48) and knocked out my written before I EVER started flying. Now don't get me wrong - I would shop around, take a discovery flight or a flight with a friend to make sure I actually like aviation first. But once I'm set I'm diving right into a ground school and knocking that written test out of the park. I'm talking a 90% minimum!

2. I would have applied for my aviation medical certificate before my first lesson. Aviation medical certificates are cheap, but waiting for them can cost you money by easily putting your flight training off track or on hold altogether. I was very lucky and had

no medical issues but you would be amazed at how the smallest things can set off red flags in the FAA's system. It could cause a hangup lasting MONTHS! Take the medical exam early so you can work through any of these potential problem areas early on.

3. Once I had my written test passed and medical certificate in hand, I would have started my training. However I wouldn't have gone at it as "willy nilly" as I did many years ago. I would have sat down with my CFI, used a clear outline/syllabus and listed my goals and objectives.

4. During my training I would have continued to learn and push myself. Just because I had that written test doesn't mean my ground studies stop. They just change direction as I begin to chair fly more and prep for that big checkride day! The studies allow you first to understand the material and then be able to apply these concepts to real life flying. It is called application and correlation. If you go on to get the CFI you will realize very quickly that this needs to happen when learning as a student.

It's so important you keep that training of yours on track. Knock out as much as you can ahead of time on the ground. Please sit down with your CFI and define your objectives and goals so everyone is on the same page.

TRANSFER OF RESPONSIBILITY

As you progress in your flight training, more and more responsibility will be given to you. This is a good thing!

For example, early on your CFI might start out helping with the radios. Yet as you progress in your training it's important that you notice more and more responsibility start to head your way, such as taking over the radios.

Quick Story

Many years ago I was flying with one of my favorite students because he really had a heart of gold and a passion for aviation.

He had come from another instructor who wasn't very good about transferring responsibility. His old instructor would always be dancing on the pedals helping ever so slightly and never hesitated to grab the yoke and let my "new to me" student fly or land the airplane himself, let alone solo!

So one day while doing pattern work with this student he was making AWESOME landings and after each one he'd say "Were you touching the controls?" "Nope, dude that was all you," I'd reply.

Yet he still wouldn't believe me. His negative experience with his old CFI had really made an impact.

He never knew when he was flying and when he wasn't.

So after what he thought was our last landing he asked the question again for what felt like the 700th time! "Jason, were you on the controls?"

As I unbuckled my seatbelt and opened the door I said "No. And to prove it to you, I'm leaving. Go do three landings just like you've been doing all along."

It literally took me getting out in the middle of the runway (the plane was stopped- don't worry!) for my student to realize he was the one truly flying the airplane.

It's important that you can actually see and track a transfer of responsibility from your CFI.

WHAT EVERY PILOT SHOULD OWN

It's easy in aviation to buy every shiny object that is placed in front of us. In this section I will outline what I believe are the essentials for your ground work and flying.

Study Material and Pilot Supplies

Again I can't say it enough, if you are not inside some sort of Online Ground School, I highly encourage you to join one. Of course I'd love for you to check out the one we put together (learn more on page 48)

As far as books go, the MUST HAVE books are a FAR/AIM, ACS, and Airplane Flying Handbook. From there, I would supplement my knowledge as necessary. If you're struggling with landings, pick up a book on landings. If you need help understanding what the FAR/

AIM is saying, well, there are books on that as well.

Some other essential items include:

• *E6B Flight Computer*

• *Plotter*

• *Local Sectional Chart*

• *Local US Chart Supplement (Formally AFD)*

• *Kneeboard*

These are just some basics! You by no means need to run out today and get all this stuff. Buy it as you need it to prevent being overwhelmed. Your CFI will be a great resource for either borrowing these items from or telling you when you need to obtain them.

Notice what's not on this list. I didn't put a flight bag. Yes, you do need some sort of "flight bag" to carry everything around in but it doesn't have to be an official aviation bag (sorry to all my business friends who manufacture flight bags). The honest truth is that any duffel bag will do. It doesn't have to be specifically made for aviation. But you will need a bag of some sort.

What else did I not mention? What about a headset? Yes, one day you will need one, but a headset is a SERIOUS purchase that costs anywhere from a few hundred bucks to upward of a few thousand!

Rent headsets, try out friend's headsets, but don't buy until you know you've got the perfect one and read every review possible about it. This is your future hearing you're investing in after all! Don't hesitate to shop the market.

Quick Story on Headsets...

My hearing stinks. It's due in part to my 10,000 hours of flight time, as about 6,000 of those hours were flown with an old, cheap, headset. The headset (like most back then) used "passive technology," which means they were just big, loud, headphones.

Between engine noise, blaring ATC radio calls, and that terrible "screech" noise that's made when two pilots key the mic at the same time (a sound which you'll learn all too well during your training), my headset was slowly ruining my hearing.

This isn't meant to scare you off from flying. It's meant to encourage you to shop around and make a smart investment in your headset.

I personally now fly with the Bose A20 headset.

There is no greater investment to make in aviation than the longevity of your hearing.

"PASS YOUR CHECKRIDE OR I'LL PAY FOR IT"

Our #1 Rated Online Ground School Has Created Over 12,000 Private Pilots and Still To This Day Maintains a 99% Pass Rate

ONLINE GROUND SCHOOL MEMBERS RECEIVE:

• Over 600HD Flight Training Videos

• Customized Written Test Prep

• LIVE Weekly Workshop Webinars

• LIVE Q&A Sessions

• LIVE Mock Checkrides

• FAA Written Test Bootcamp

• Interact With Jason Each Week

• Mobile Friendly - Learn On The Go

"Using a lot of what I learned in Jason's online ground school and webinars, I was able to score a 95% on my FAA written exam, and was told by the DPE that my performance on the oral part of my checkride was one of the best he'd seen in a few years. I also highly recommend his many supplemental publications, as they are full of information and tips to make you a better pilot. Going into both exams, I felt confident in my preparation and knowledge base, I truly believe that MzeroA played a very large part in my success. I can't thank you enough!"
Jeff Fisher, Private Pilot

"PRIVATE PILOT BLUEPRINT READERS SAVE 30% ON ANY ONLINE GROUND SCHOOL MEMBERSHIP! VISIT THE URL BELOW TO SIGNUP AND ENTER PROMO CODE BELOW TO SAVE 30%

BLUEPRINT30

GroundSchoolAcademy.com

CHAPTER 4
FLYING SOLO

"THERE ARE OLD PILOTS AND BOLD PILOTS BUT
NO OLD BOLD PILOTS" - PILOT WISDOM

WHAT TO EXPECT ON YOUR FIRST SOLO

Believe it or not, you may not know when your big day will be. I do my best as a flight instructor to let a student know they are doing well and getting close to solo (so they can mentally prepare), but not leading on too much with a specific date.

Weather changes, winds shift, traffic in the pattern varies. You never know when the perfect day to solo is. Sometimes it just happens.

I made the mistake once of telling my student when she was going to solo. Her landings were really coming along and her confidence in the plane really showed. I made the mistake of saying "If you fly like that tomorrow I'll solo you!" Big mistake on my part.

She went out and told all her family and friends that she would be soloing tomorrow. Most of them even showed up at the airport! A <u>BIG</u> no-no in my book. You don't need the added pressure of loved ones at your first solo. Now the pressure was on me to solo her!

Needless to say it just wasn't her day. Have you ever just had an off day? Well double that due to the pressure of friends and family watching and your mind racing about your solo. Her landings that day were nowhere close to the quality she'd done in days previous.

I had to be the bad guy and say I'm sorry but I can't solo you today. Dejected and embarrassed in front of her friends my student never called me back. I was fired, because I broke two CFI rules: Never tell a student the exact day of their solo and never encourage friends and family to show up at the airport to watch.

Call me a "party pooper" all you want but realize that your mind already has enough going through it. The last thing you need is the added pressure of knowing when you'll solo, and having family there cheering you on. I felt as if I had to solo my student because I made that promise and because the family was there. It's hard to standby your beliefs and know when to say "no".

Your First Solo

You will never forget the day of your solo. I usually try to catch a student by surprise and just hop out of the airplane and say "have fun and be safe." That way they don't have too long to process what just happened and get nervous.

There is no FAA-mandated minimum number of hours to solo, just an age (16 years of age). There is also no mandated script or syllabus to follow for your first solo. But what is common is that the student will take a few laps around the pattern - sometimes one, but often three full-stop/taxiback landings

I try to solo my students at an uncontrolled airport

although this is not required by any means, It's just my preference. I like it when the traffic pattern is dead and I can stand out by the runway with my handheld radio and cheer them on each step of the way.

When it's all said and done I usually let them taxi it on home and I meet them back at the hanger where we do the traditional t-shirt cutting.

Why do we cut t-shirts?

Back in the golden ages of flying when training was done in a more traditional aircraft like a Piper Cub, radios were not as prevalent. So in a cub the seating arrangement is whats called "tandem seating" (forward and aft). So your instructor sat behind you and would yell certain commands over the airplane noise. If you think the airplane is a terrible classroom, imagine being in a noisy Piper Cub with no headsets!

When your instructor wanted you to head back to

the airport or turn a certain direction he would pull on your shirt tail. A pull on the left of your shirt tail meant a turn to the left.

So the cutting of the shirt tail signifies that you no longer need a flight instructor telling you what to do and where to turn.

A few notes before you solo

Remember that when your instructor steps out of that airplane it's going to perform like a rocket! I'm close to 200lbs. When I get out of our Cessna 150 or even the Cessna 172, my students notice an instant difference on takeoff.

Where it really matters is landing. Without that extra weight, you'll have a tendency to float down the runway leaving your point of intended landing a few hundred feet behind you. This is why it's advisable to do full stop taxi back landings as opposed to touch and go's on your first solo.

Remember that your CFI would not have signed you off to solo if he/she didn't believe you were ready. After all, they are responsible for you, the aircraft, and their certificate. Soloing a student is a BIG responsibility!

Trust their judgement and reward that CFI with confidence on your part. But remember - there is a big difference between confidence and cockiness.

As you get closer to your solo start wearing older t-shirts or bringing extra ones. :)

BEYOND THE SOLO

Once you've soloed and have proven you have mastered the art of entering, working in, and exiting the traffic pattern, your CFI will send you out for more confidence-building flights.

Usually I'll let my students solo a bit more around the traffic pattern to build confidence and eventually I'll let them show up to the airport without me there and handle everything.

It's on that flight that I let them venture into the practice area just like we've always done to practice their flight maneuvers.

I make sure that they fully understand how to exit the pattern and reenter. They will also conduct a proper pre-maneuver checklist.

The Pre-maneuver Checklist

Before EVERY flight maneuver you perform there should be a set pre-maneuver checklist that gets conducted. I teach my students the acronym "PARC"

P - Pre-maneuver Checklist

A - Area to Land

R - Radio Call

C - Clearing Turns

Pre-Maneuver Checklist - This is usually a flow checklist (done from memory, then verified on the actual checklist). I just want to make sure my aircraft is in the proper configuration and ready to go for whatever maneuver I'm doing. In most aircraft I fly (usually a Cessna 150 or 172) it goes like this.

"Starting on the floor. Fuel selector valve **ON BOTH**. *Working my way straight up to mixture* **RICH**. *Across to my throttle* **SET**. *Then carb heat* **AS NEEDED**. *All the way across to my primer* **IN / LOCKED**. *Engine gauges verified* **GOOD**."

I'm just trying to make sure everything is good to go on my airplane before I conduct this maneuver.

NOTE: When you show up to the airport for the first time and ask your CFI if you should do a pre-maneuver checklist before you start say a steep turn or slow flight they are going to be REALLY impressed.

Area To Land - What if something goes wrong? What if the engine quits halfway through this maneuver? I want to have an emergency area to land, chosen ahead of time, so I know exactly where I'm going. Keep in mind when looking for this area before the maneuver that the best landing area might be behind you or below you.

Radio Call - Most (not all) practice areas have a set frequency but if yours does, this is when you'd make a radio call letting everyone else in the area know what you're doing, where you're at, and at what altitude you'll be maneuvering.

Clearing Turns - A clearing turn is a simple turn 90 degrees to the left (that's a 90 degree heading change not bank!), then right 90 degrees, back to your original heading. During that time we're looking outside, above us and below us, for other traffic or obstacles. Clearing turns are always done last because after you've gone through this PARC acronym, chances are good you've travelled a little bit and there may be different traffic in the area. Clearing turns are also always done to the left first, because in a perfect world, if an aircraft were to overtake you and pass you they should always pass off to your right side. So assuming that is a possibility, we make our turn to the left first to prevent blindly turning into someone.

PERFECTING YOUR FLIGHT MANEUVERS

Each flight maneuver has its set purpose and function to help you ultimately improve various aspects of your flight training. For example, the maneuver slow flight is geared toward helping a student make better landings, believe it or not.

MzeroA.com was first in pioneering the use of externally mounted cameras to capture all angles of flight training inside and outside of the cockpit.

I encourage you to check out some of our great free content on YouTube by visiting our channel at

YouTube.com/MzeroAFlightTraining

WHY WE PRACTICE EACH FLIGHT MANEUVER

I'm a big advocate of helping student pilots understand why we do each maneuver. Very early on in my training I had no idea why certain maneuvers were required.

My CFI would just tell me "do this," and we did it. I never really had an understanding of why.

As someone who asks A LOT of questions, this was hard for me.

Here's the scoop: This chapter will make a lot more sense to someone who's at least taken a ground school or a few lessons. So if these next few pages are hard to grasp don't worry. I encourage you to use the link on the previous page to get a better visual.

Steep Turns - Steep turns are a maneuver where the pilot attempts to maintain a constant altitude while turning the airplane 360 degrees at a 45 degree bank angle. You're required to maintain + or - 100 feet from your start altitude and roll out within + or - 10 degrees of your original heading.

We practice steep turns to learn how to take the airplane through its paces. We can use this maneuver to avoid obstacles or other airplanes if on a collision course. It's about taking our aircraft to the extreme while maintaining our altitude and airspeed.

During steeps turns, one of two things will happen. Your eyes will be either glued inside or outside the cockpit. Eyes inside the cockpit (only looking at your instrument panel) is not good because, after all, aren't we pursuing a VFR (Visual Flight Rules) license? Eyes inside also means you're more than likely fixating on one or two instruments while the rest are going haywire.

Looking only outside, although the better option, is not

great either. You want to develop a balance.

I prefer to think of most of these flight maneuvers as 80/20: 80% of my time spent looking outside the cockpit with 20% looking inside at my flight instruments confirming what I already know from looking outside.

Slow Flight - Slow flight was a maneuver I struggled to understand. I would think to myself, "Why do I want to get this airplane so close to a stall in the first place?" It didn't make sense to me.

Then someone explained to me that right before we touchdown we are effectively in slow flight. It finally clicked.

Slow flight has two variations, "clean" (no flaps) and "dirty" (with flaps). The objective is to maintain the recommended airspeed (stalling airspeeds in various configurations) while maintaining your altitude and heading. Oh and by the way- you can't stall or that would be a bust on the checkride.

Similar to steep turns you must maintain + or - 100ft from your start altitude and + or - 10 degrees on your heading. You also must maintain +10 and - 0 of your recommended airspeed.

I am a big advocate of practicing slow flight on a regular basis. In fact, I believe you cannot be truly great at landings until you've mastered slow flight.

Stalls - There are several different types of stalls but for the sake of this book, we'll cover two: Power-on, sometimes called a departure or takeoff stall, and power-off, sometimes called an approach or landing stall.

I want you to get one thing committed to memory: We practice stalls to practice recoveries.

We don't want to learn how to stall. That is silly. We want to learn how to recover and avoid stalls altogether.

Most checkride examiners don't care how you get into the stall; they care more about how efficiently you recover.

Power-On Stalls: In a power-on stall, you are simulating a stall during takeoff. You've pitched too high and failed to notice the decreasing airspeed and blaring stall warning horn or light, not to mention the sloppy controls and aerodynamic buffeting. Before you know it, the airplane can no longer maintain flight and the nose drops.

This is where the grading starts. How fast do you help get that nose down, throttle full, and airplane flying again? That is what an examiner wants to know.

Power-Off Stalls: A power-off stall is simulating a stall while you're coming into land. Flaps are down, airspeed back to idle. Suddenly you think you're a 787 as you pitch back as if to "flare." (This is a word I encourage you to remove from your vocabulary. Our online ground school members know why.)

The airspeed continues to decrease rapidly, warning indications follow and the airplane's nose breaks forward. How quickly you add power, bring the flaps to an appropriate setting and get that airplane back flying directly relates to the grade your examiner will give you.

Ground Reference Maneuvers - There are three different ground reference maneuvers for the private and sport pilot ratings: Turns around a point, s-turns, and rectangular course.

All are designed to do one thing: Teach you how the wind interacts with our airplane and our course across the ground. Since they are called *ground* maneuvers, you should spend most of your time looking at the ground. You will be looking for other aircraft in the area and remaining cognizant of possible landing areas in case the engine quits.

With each maneuver you are referencing something fixed on the ground. Let's use turns around a point as an example.

I choose an object such as a barn, lone tree in a field or two roads out in the country that cross at ninety degrees. I am looking for something stationary on the ground. I fly a complete circle (360 degrees) around that barn from roughly 800 feet above the ground while maintaining not only my altitude, but also the distance from the barn. The FAA recommends 600 to 1000 feet above the ground for all ground reference maneuvers.

Sounds easy? Well, not really.

As you turn, the wind impacts the airplane at different angles, pushing you and pulling you from your barn that you are to maintain the same distance around.

You as the pilot, need to learn how to adjust your bank angle to literally "ride the wind" in some cases.

Short Field Operations - We practice what are called short field takeoffs and landings. What we're simulating is a takeoff or landing at a shorter-than-normal runway. Anything under 2,500ft is considered short(ish) for most of our training aircraft (172's or PA28's).

Soft Field Operations - We also train to land on surfaces other than pavement. We often assume that a soft field landing means grass. But it really could be anything, for example dirt or gravel..

The funny thing about soft field takeoffs and landings is this: We practice them on the pavement. Does that make any sense? I didn't get to do my first actual soft field landing until I was well into my commercial pilot training.

Don't let your flight school tell you, "Oh, our insurance doesn't allow that." As someone who's insured with all the major aviation insurance companies, I can tell you there is no such rule. Do yourself a favor and find someone who will take you to a real grass strip. It's an awesome experience.

Emergency Procedures - A good portion of our training is spent on "what if" scenarios. Although the chances are one in a million, you want to make sure you have all your bases covered. Be ready to practice things like engine failures inflight, engine fires on start, lost radio communications procedures and lost (navigational) procedures.

Hey Jason,

I wanted to thank you for the great private pilot audio book, and all your podcast information. I passed my checkride with flying colors yesterday, at 43.2 hours the examiner was quite impressed with how much I knew during the oral, and inflight. Actually during the debrief he was scratching his head for things to talk about.

I truly believe the outcome would have been much different without the information I gathered from you, so I thank you very much and I have been passing your web site along to

students I have been meeting, keep up the good work I look forward to listening to the instrument rating audiobook next.

- Trip Harrington

CHAPTER 5
THE WRITTEN TEST

"TRULY SUPERIOR PILOTS ARE THOSE THAT USE
THEIR SUPERIOR JUDGMENT TO AVOID THOSE
SITUATIONS WHERE THEY MIGHT HAVE TO USE
THEIR SUPERIOR SKILLS" - PILOT WISDOM

WHAT IS THE WRITTEN TEST?

The written test is a 60-question (multiple-choice) knowledge test. It covers all subjects outlined in section 61.105 of the Federal Aviation Regulations. COUGH COUGH! (That's a polite way of saying "Go read it!")

By now you know what a good instructor is and how to find one. With that, you must trust your instructor. They know you well enough to tell you if you're ready to take the test or not. At this point you shouldn't have more than 0.5 hours logged. <u>Do not start your flight training before you take the written test!</u> An introductory flight is recommended, but nothing more.

I <u>promise</u> that written test will be the monkey on your back until you get it done. What's the best way to knock it out ASAP? Let me share with you my secrets.

PREPPING FOR THE TEST

For the written exam, preparation is key. Study and become familiar with all subjects listed in FAR 61.105. Be sure to take practice tests regularly. Any high quality ground school program (like our online ground school) has the ability to allow students to practice as many times as they want. You can actually take practice tests using the REAL FAA question bank inside our online ground school!

However, it's so essential to have a thorough understanding of the material, and not to just memorize questions and answers. It is one thing to know what the answers are to particular questions on various subjects; but the wording on the written can in some cases trick people. You must know how to apply what you already know to any given scenario or question. It is a KNOWLEDGE test, NOT a "who can memorize the most questions" test.

Take advantage of all the FREE material MzeroA has to offer. Although no one is perfect, there have been several people who have scored an impressive 100% on their written exam. Some of them are MzeroA Online Ground School members!. It is possible. It should be noted that it's unwise to go in for your written test unsure, or with any weak areas in any subject. This can be easily avoided by studying, and even teaching your flight instructor what you've learned. Information on some of the very subjects you will be tested on is FREE to you by just subscribing to MzeroA Flight Training on YouTube, Again, that is all available for FREE. (Links to these resources are published at the end of the book.)

Lastly, it is well known across the aviation community that very often, people score anywhere from 5-10 points lower on their actual written compared to the practice test scores. Just because you're scoring in the high 80 percentile on your practice tests doesn't necessarily mean you're going to score that on the actual written. To be completely sure you'll pass the exam without a hitch, reconsider your preparation tactics and work closely with your instructor. Don't go about this on your own and be sure to take the usual 5-10 "test day anxiety" point drop.

WHAT TO BRING AND HOW TO PREPARE

You'd be surprised at where you can take your FAA Written Test. Most airports and local colleges have testing centers. Search for a "CATS Testing Center" to find the closest location to take your test.

Call the test center for the price of the test, and ask what forms of payment are accepted.

You will need to bring a government-issued identification card, such as a driver's license, military I.D., etc., and your endorsement to take the test! Which is provided via a passing score in our Online Ground School.

Materials you will use during the test include: A simple four-function calculator (no phones or scientific calculators are allowed), an E6B Flight Computer, a navigation plotter and at least two pencils.

The test center might tell you they have all you'll need and to just come with the required documents. Bring your own test taking material anyway.

Side Note: It's important to realize that the score you get on your written test will directly relate to the difficulty on the oral section of the checkride. What do I mean?

If you march into the checkride with a 71% score on your written exam, the examiner is going to look at that and think, "Either this guy is a poor test taker or has some serious gaps in his/her training."

On the flip side, march in with anything above a 90% and your checkride examiner will know that you mean business and know your stuff. Strive for the best score possible.

Online ground school members get the benefit of "Pass Your Written or I'll Pay For It." Ground School members also receive their written test endorsement from us. So even if you don't have an instructor we can endorse you to take the test.

Jason,

Thank You for your video tips as well as the" Pass Your Private Pilot Checkride" book. I passed my checkride at 42.7 hrs. and your book gave me the confidence. My CFII told me I was ready, but your book helped me solidify that by giving me what I really needed to focus on.

Thanks again!

Brian Lewis

P52/AZ

CHAPTER 6
THE CHECKRIDE

"IF IT'S RED OR DUSTY DON'T TOUCH IT!"

- PILOT WISDOM

WHAT IS THE CHECKRIDE?

It's the big day, and the final exam has arrived. To help calm your nerves I always tell my students that it's their first flight as a private pilot and that the examiner sitting next to them is just their first passenger.

The checkride consists of an oral exam (verbal question asking and explanations) plus a flight exam. Count on both being AT LEAST an hour and usually more.

Remember one thing: The examiner wants you to pass. They have no quota to meet as designated pass/fail ratio. They are there simply to see if you'll be a safe pilot and an efficient pilot. You will be an advocate of general aviation from that time forward.

WHAT TO BRING AND HOW TO PREPARE

Well the time has come, and it's the day before you're checkride. This is a serious endeavor, but there's no need for fear. The great flight instructor you've chosen using the tips in this book would not have endorsed you for a checkride unprepared.

Most examiners will set some boundaries before the flight, and your instructor will most likely know what the boundaries of a particular examiner are. That is to say don't show up to your checkride with the whole plan on your iPad, an electronic E6B, and no back-ups in place at all. Some examiners don't mind you using an electronic E6B. But, as a good pilot, you need to know how to do everything the "old-fashioned" way. Most of the time the examiner will say, "The battery on your iPad just died." and if you can't go on without them, then...

Don't forget to bring your exam fee, which is usually around $500 - $600 bucks! YIKES! The best part is every examiner I know always asks for cash which I find funny considering they are a government subcontractor but that's another story.

Get insurance on your checkride. Our Online Ground School Gold Members receive my "Pass Your Checkride or I'll Pay For It" guarantee. We've maintained a 99.6% pass rating for 12,000 students and counting.

ENJOYING THE RIDE

As mentioned above, the examiner is your first passenger. Treat him or her that way. Your instructor has a certain pass rate they want or need to maintain, so they would never put you up for a test if you weren't ready, that is for sure.

Stay relaxed and be the pilot in command. You will do fine on your big test day.

MY #1 TIP FOR YOU RIGHT NOW

If I was in your shoes I'd learn everything I can on the ground. I wish I would have done that. I was my own worst enemy and I don't want you to make the same mistake I did by pushing ground work to the back burner.

If I were you, I'd go back and take action on all the free videos I mentioned at URLs throughout this book.

If you've enjoyed this book and believe my real-world teaching style works for you, I strongly recommend you join our #1 Rated Online Ground School. If you think this was good, wait until you see the 400+ videos in addition to the weekly LIVE webinars and mock checkrides we do.

Visit <u>GroundSchoolAcademy.com</u> to learn more

Have a question for Jason and the team? Want to share your success story with us? Call us at 855-737-1200 or shoot us an email by going to:

MzeroA.com/Support

QUICK REFERENCE URLS FOUND IN THIS BOOK

We produce 4 different Aviation Flight Training Podcasts as well.

Search iTunes for

The Private Pilot Podcast
The Instrument Pilot Podcast
The Commercial Pilot Podcast
The CFI Podcast

Obviously a great resource is MzeroA.com. Between our YouTube videos and everything else you're going to love it and get some much value out of the entire thing.

My premise is this. If you LOVE the free videos and content I put on MzeroA.com you're going to LOVE the paid content inside the Online Ground School.

You can learn more about our #1 rated Online Ground School at GroundSchoolAcademy.com

Be sure to use the promo code found on page 48 to save

30% on your next purchase at <u>MzeroA.com</u>

Thank you SO MUCH for taking the time to read this book. I can already tell you're going to be a GREAT pilot. Anyone who is willing to take the time and read this book cover to cover like yourself is a truly GREAT pilot.

Keep learning all you can and keep me posted on your success. I hope to play a small role in your BIG success!

Enjoy it

and remember...

That a GOOD Pilot is ALWAYS Learning!

See Ya,